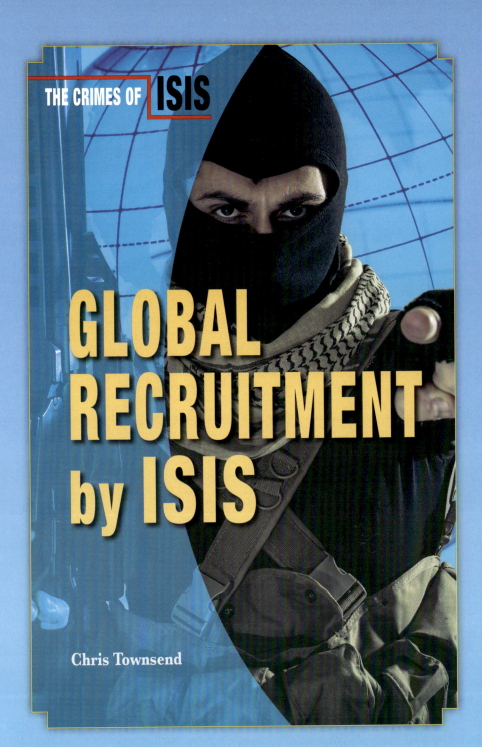

THE CRIMES OF ISIS

GLOBAL RECRUITMENT by ISIS

Chris Townsend

Enslow Publishing

101 W. 23rd Street
Suite 240
New York, NY 10011
USA

enslow.com

Published in 2018 by Enslow Publishing, LLC.
101 W. 23rd Street, Suite 240, New York, NY 10011

Copyright © 2018 by Enslow Publishing, LLC.

All rights reserved.

No part of this book may be reproduced by any means without the written permission of the publisher.

Library of Congress Cataloging-in-Publication Data

Names: Townsend, Chris (Writer on the Middle East), author.
Title: Global recruitment by ISIS / by Chris Townsend.
Description: New York, NY : Enslow Publishing, 2018. | Series: The crimes of ISIS | Includes bibliographical references and index. | Audience: Grades 7–12.
Identifiers: LCCN 2017017715 | ISBN 9780766092129 (library bound) | ISBN 9780766095816 (paperback)
Subjects: LCSH: IS (Organization)—Juvenile literature. |
  Terrorists—Recruiting—Juvenile literature. | Jihad—Juvenile literature.
  | Terrorism—Religious aspects—Islam—Juvenile literature.
Classification: LCC HV6433.I722 T69 2018 | DDC 363.325—dc23
LC record available at https://lccn.loc.gov/2017017715

Printed in the United States of America

To Our Readers: We have done our best to make sure all websites in this book were active and appropriate when we went to press. However, the author and the publisher have no control over and assume no liability for the material available on those websites or on any websites they may link to. Any comments or suggestions can be sent by email to customerservice@enslow.com.

Photo Credits: Cover, p. 1 oneinchpunch/Shuttertsock.com; cover, p. 1 (globe) photastic/Shuttertsock.com; pp. 4, 18–19, 21, 29, 52–53 Anadolu Agency/Getty Images; pp. 6–7, 50–51, 80–81 AFP/Getty Images; p. 10 Ahmad Al-Rubaye/AFP/Getty Images; pp. 12–13 amer ghazzal/Alamy Stock Photo; pp. 14–15 JM Lopez/AFP/Getty Images; pp. 24–25 Mohammed Abed/AFP/Getty Images; p. 27 Chip Somodevilla/Getty Images; p. 32 Win McNamee/Getty Images; pp. 36–37 Rex Features/AP Images; pp. 38–39 Press Association/AP Images; pp. 42–43 Martyn Evans/Alamy Stock Photo; pp. 44–45, 76–77 TASS/Getty Images; p. 47 Mir Hamid/Daily Dawn/Gamma-Rapho/Getty Images; pp. 56–57 Emmanuel Arewa/AFP/Getty Images; p. 61 NurPhoto/Getty Images; pp. 64–65 David Ramos/Getty Images; pp. 68–69 Gina Ferazzi/Los Angeles Times/Getty Images; pp. 70–71 Ahmad Gharabli/AFP/Getty Images; pp. 74–75 © AP Images; pp. 78–79 Drew Angerer/Getty Images; pp. 84–85 Musa Al Shaer/AFP/Getty Images.

CONTENTS

	Introduction	5
1	Come to Jihad	9
2	Tell Me a Tale	20
3	Spinning the Web	31
4	The Spreading Darkness	46
5	Terror on the Homefront	59
6	Draining the Swamp	73
	Chapter Notes	89
	Glossary	96
	Further Reading	100
	Index	102

People march in Gaza, Palestine, demanding a return to an Islamic caliphate, which, prior to ISIS's declaration, last existed nearly one hundred years ago.

INTRODUCTION

When Abu Bakr al-Baghdadi called all Muslims to join the self-proclaimed Islamic State and fight jihad, tens of thousands answered the call from all over the globe. This book explores the formation of the Islamic State and how the organization went about recruiting an army to challenge the world order. It will explore how the Islamic State used traditional recruitment methods, such as outreach through mosques and local influencers, as well as more modern tactics, like social media and smartphone apps, to amass its following and will discuss what type of follower each mode of recruitment attracted.

Depending on whom you ask, the name of the group is ISIS, ISIL, IS, or Da'esh. That we can't agree on what to call the group highlights one of the challenges the world has found in addressing the problem. They call themselves Doulat al-Islamiya fil-Iraq wa Shams (Da'esh). It translates literally to the Islamic State in Iraq and the Levant (ISIL). The Levant is a French name for the region that encompasses modern day Syria, Jordan, Lebanon, Israel, and Palestine. Some prefer to just

Abu Bakr al-Baghdadi, shown here at a mosque in Mosul, Iraq, announced the founding of the caliphate, or the Islamic State of Iraq and Syria, in June 2014.

leave Shams untranslated or translate it incorrectly as Syria, giving us the acronym ISIS, though the group primarily refers to itself now as simply the Islamic State (IS). Despite the fact that ISIS is not the most correct acronym for the group, it is the most common. For simplicity's sake, ISIS is the name that will be used in this book.

The group began as a branch of al-Qaeda, the terrorist organization from Afghanistan that carried out the attacks on September 11, 2001. Its founder, a Jordanian named Abu Musab al-Zarqawi, named his group al-Qaeda in Iraq. After his death the group was reformed as the Islamic State in Iraq. In 2014 the group formally declared itself a caliphate and changed its name to ISIS.

The group has been able to take advantage of the instability that followed American troops' withdrawal from Iraq in 2011. As Syria fell into chaos to the west, the group was able to expand and lay claim to a physical state of its own, ignoring the borders between the two halves of the fledgling state.

From its bloody beginning, the group has imposed its strict and violent interpretations of Islam on those caught in its lands. From the desert, the call went out for warriors to come join ISIS. Many fighters heard the call and traveled to Iraq and Syria to fight for ISIS. Others waged war at home, attacking their fellow citizens in countries around the world. As believers across the globe continue to find ways to spread their message of hate and attract new followers to their evil version of Islam, even more people are working to stop them. If the world can stop the flow of new believers to ISIS, the terrorist organization will eventually die.

COME TO JIHAD

"I'm sorry. I love you. I've decided to leave and I won't be coming back."

In what he expected to be his last communication with his parents, Mo Dakhlalla wrote these words in a letter before heading to the airport to join ISIS in Syria. By all accounts, Mo was like any other college student. After a whirlwind romance with another student who expressed an interest in becoming Muslim, or a follower of Islam, Mo found himself drawn into the online world of terror. Jaelyn, his new girlfriend, surprised him by converting to the faith and adopting a very conservative dress style that included a *niqab*, a total body covering that leaves only the eyes exposed. In her effort to learn more about her new faith, Jaelyn turned to the internet, where she found and introduced Mo to recruitment videos from ISIS. Mo found the arguments in the videos about the fledgling Islamic State, and its complaints about the West, convincing. Angered by the list of grievances against the West and inspired to help establish a community of Muslims, he and Jaelyn reached out to the group.

The two married in secret and began making plans with an online recruiter to join ISIS. They communicated frequently with their recruiter about their future role in ISIS. After leaving notes for their families the young couple went to the airport to catch a flight to Turkey and then cross the border into neighboring Syria. As they boarded the flight, the couple was stopped by the FBI and arrested. Their online contact turned out to have been an FBI agent working to identify people trying to join ISIS.[1]

Alex (an assumed name to protect her identity) was bored and lonely. From the relative isolation of her grandparents' farm she went looking for information about a beheading video that had captured the media's attention and instead found an online circle of friends. Soon, these friends were speaking with her all

An Iraqi soldier walks past a mural showing the ISIS flag in a town south of Mosul, Iraq, once an ISIS stronghold. Mosul was retaken by Iraqi forces in early 2017.

ISLAM

Islam is a religion that was started in the seventh century by a man named Muhammad who claimed that an angel of God had revealed to him the one true religion. Over the next twenty-two years, Muhammad continued to receive these revelations. Islam means "submission" in Arabic, and this would be the cornerstone of the new faith. A follower of Islam is called a Muslim (literally, one who submits). There are five central responsibilities for Muslims, known as the Pillars of Islam. They include confession that there is only one god, tithing to the poor, fasting, prayer five times a day, and a pilgrimage to Mecca, the holiest site in the world to Muslims. The new religion would sweep the region and a large portion of the world over the next nine hundred years, spreading its influence as far as Spain, which was known as Andalusia at the time. After the death of Muhammad, his revelations were collected into a book called the Quran. The Quran, along with the Sunna (stories about how the prophet lived) and the Hadith (sayings of the prophet), is the basis of the religion's beliefs, although there are disagreements between Muslims about the relative importance of each.

the time and sending gifts. Intrigued, she began to explore her new friends' faith, and eventually converted to Islam. She downloaded an app for her smartphone that sent her a daily message with sayings attributed to the Islamic prophet Muhammad. Eventually, she began nightly lessons about her new faith from an online teacher. The packages became more frequent and began to include pamphlets explaining the role and responsibilities of

ISIS supporters use social media platforms, such as Twitter, to reach out and recruit new followers. Though they are frequently banned, new accounts appear online daily.

women in her new faith. Then came an offer of marriage and plane tickets to meet her betrothed.

Fortunately, Alex never flew to meet her future husband. Concerned by changes in the girl's behavior, her grandmother asked for her social media passwords and was stunned by what

she found. The family, shaken by their near miss, contacted the FBI. Despite promising her family she'd stop, Alex admits to still periodically communicating with her online friends.[2]

ANSWERING THE CALL

Alex and Mo are not isolated incidents. While they were unsuccessful in their efforts to join ISIS, estimates are that forty thousand people from one hundred countries have gone to Iraq and Syria to join ISIS, including hundreds of Americans and thousands of Europeans.[3] Who would give up a life of comfort in the West for the barren, hot, war-torn deserts of Iraq and Syria? It would be easy to dismiss those who choose to join the fight as mentally unstable or uneducated, but studies have shown that neither is true. Efforts to categorize risk factors for radicalization have been largely inconclusive. While there are some characteristics that are overrepresented in the cases, like second- or third-generation immigrants, low-level criminality, and recent conversion to Islam, for every factor there are exceptions that meet none of these categories. In fact, Martha Crenshaw noted that the "outstanding common characteristic of terrorists is their normality."[4]

Undoubtedly, some are inspired by the violent videos and messages of ISIS and find their way to Syria and Iraq to join the jihad, or holy war. These recruits revel in the violent beheadings and executions and want to participate in the violence themselves. These criminals and psychopaths use the beliefs of the group as an excuse to act out their sick fantasies of violence against others. Violence and glorious infamy motivate these recruits, and Iraq and Syria have become their playgrounds.

Others have expressed a desire to belong to a community of believers. When ISIS claimed the city of Mosul, it established the caliphate, a religious state for all Muslims. Under the watchful eye of ISIS, religious law would be enforced according to the group's interpretations of the religious texts of Islam. The caliphate harkens back to the political and religious empire that came after Muhammad established the religion. In fact, the term "caliphate" comes from the Arabic word meaning "to succeed," or "follow behind." At its simplest, it represents the political body set up to rule the original Islamic State established by Muhammad's successors until it was officially disbanded in 1924 by Mustafa Kemal Ataturk, the president of Turkey. When ISIS declared Abu Bakr al-Baghdadi to be caliph of the newly formed Islamic State, they were laying claim to a long and storied history of Muslim conquest and rule. For some, this environment represents the ideal situation for devout Muslims who wish to live in accordance with the tenets of their faith.

A Kurdish Peshmerga fighter fires at ISIS combatants east of Mosul in 2014. Though Iraqi Kurdistan is an independent region in northern Iraq, the Peshmerga have frequently led the fight against ISIS, especially in nearby Mosul, Iraq.

Many fighters came to join ISIS out of a sense of obligation to defend Muslims and their land. In his early addresses, al-Baghdadi and another ISIS member, Abu Muhammad al-Adnani, called for all Muslims to come to the restored caliphate and fight on behalf of all oppressed Muslims, both

JIHAD

"Jihad" is a complex term scholars of Islam have argued about since day one. The most common interpretation of the term in popular context is as "holy war." This definition is not without historical justification but ignores that of the forty-one references to the word in the Quran, only twelve equate the term with war.[5] In some cases, it is translated as an internal struggle to follow the word of God, and in others it is stated literally as a violent clash to defend the faith. The word comes from the Arabic *jahada,* which means to struggle. Jihad is a noun form of the verb meaning "struggling" or "striving." Fundamentalists argue that jihad is a sacred duty that requires them to fight against all nonbelievers, earning these fundamentalists the label of jihadists. This interpretation becomes increasingly dangerous as their definition of nonbeliever can even include Muslims who interpret their faith differently from the jihadists' strict interpretations. In this book, the term "jihad" will be used in the modern context, as it is a central tenet of ISIS ideology and a primary motivation for many who join.

those living and those martyred in previous clashes such as the Crusades. ISIS based their call on a perceived decline of the Islamic world since its golden age, when Baghdad was considered the center of the learned world. To ISIS and its members, the Israel-Palestine conflict and the killings of Muslims in the former Soviet states all contribute to a narrative that Muslims must unite because they are under attack from every side. They constantly accuse the West of seeking to destroy Islam and all

Muslims. For these recruits, violence is a means to an end and justified by the perceived persecution of other Muslims.

Women have joined ISIS for all of the previous reasons, but overwhelmingly represent another strange category. Many come to Iraq and Syria to present themselves as brides to the fighters of ISIS. In the year following the declaration of the caliphate, around 550 Western women left their homes and families to journey to Iraq and Syria and join the jihadists.[6] The primary role for these women has been as wives of the jihadists and the mothers of future jihadists. When a woman's husband dies, she is promptly remarried to another jihadist. Stranger still is the practice of temporary marriages, where a woman is married to a fighter — in some cases to multiple fighters in a single night — to serve as his wife in what amounts to legalized prostitution.[7]

BECOMING RADICAL

There is no single path to radicalization. Radicalization is a process by which someone disagrees with the existing system and comes to believe that they are required to take action to change that system. Those who join ISIS are so varied as to defy categorization. They are wealthy and poor, intelligent and ignorant, educated and uneducated, lifelong Muslims and new converts, men and women, devout and secular, old and young, disturbed and disturbingly sane. The only common thread is the acceptance of the jihadists' central belief that there is a war between Islam and the West, and that all good Muslims have a duty to abandon the unbelievers and be part of the Islamic State.[8] This is a radical change in thought and lifestyle for most.

Since the beginning of the modern terrorist era in the 1970s, scholars have wrestled with what causes radicalization or leads to an individual committing acts like terrorism. The transformation from normal person to jihadist has been likened to a conveyor belt, an escalator, and even a "slippery slope," where an individual is moved along from stage to stage until they reach a point where they are committed to action against the system.[9] There is no agreement on the number or exact nature of steps along the journey to becoming radicalized, but the general route includes some type of grievance, a guiding narrative, and a mobilization to action.[10] While starting points and paths differ, the end result is similar regardless of the terror organization: individuals become polarized, absolutist, threat-oriented, and hateful.[11]

While it is easy to imagine someone who is caught up in the actual fight picking a side and engaging in violence, it is harder to understand why people around the globe have decided to leave their lives behind and take up the jihadist mantle. Thousands of seemingly normal people have internalized the message of ISIS and been motivated to join the group in its quest for world domination.

A SAD ENDING

Samra Kesinovic was a beautiful girl. Her family had fled war-torn Bosnia and settled in Austria where she lived a normal life. In April 2014, Samra and a friend, Sabina Selimovic, left a note for their parents that read, "Don't look for us. We will serve Allah and we will die for him." The two boarded a plane and

Three women ISIS supporters appear in court in Kenya in 2015. The women were arrested near the border between Kenya and Somalia and were accused of attempting to get to Syria to serve as ISIS brides.

soon were posting to social media from inside Syria, wearing the niqab and brandishing machine guns. After growing tired of the strict rules of the group, Samra repeatedly tried to escape. Her final note to her parents proved prophetic when a Tunisian woman who had been held with Samra reported that the young woman, known as the poster girl of ISIS, had been beaten to death with a hammer.[12]

2

TELL ME A TALE

The man in black paused at the foot of the stairs to the podium of the mosque in Mosul, Iraq. A month prior, his soldiers had swept through the city. Their previous campaign of terror and gruesome executions paid off as Iraqi soldiers crumbled in the face of the assault and fled despite possessing superior numbers and weapons. When the dust settled, ISIS controlled the city and its historic mosque. As he climbed to the podium, the man in black paused again at each step. Once at the podium, he pulled a stick from his pocket with which to clean his teeth. Anyone familiar with stories of the prophet Muhammad would recognize the man's behavior, and even his black clothes and headdress, as a mirror image of the prophet, from whom the man claimed his lineage. His speech confirmed what his clothing and demeanor suggested: the caliphate of old was restored. Abu Bakr al-Baghdadi, like his namesake, the first successor of Muhammad, laid claim to the title of caliph. His message was clear. Every Muslim had a duty to obey him as the leader of all Muslims and to join the fight against the nonbelievers.[1]

Abu Bakr al-Baghdadi, the leader of ISIS and the self-proclaimed caliph of the Islamic State, appears in a video filmed at a mosque in Iraq in 2014.

THE CALIPHATE

The word "caliphate" comes from the Arabic word *khalafa*, which means to succeed or follow behind. When the prophet Muhammad died in 632 CE, his followers were left without a leader. There was disagreement over who should lead the fledgling Islamic nation. The immediate problem was solved by the appointment of a successor, or a caliph. As Islam spread, various caliphs were selected to lead the faithful. Eventually, the faith split into two factions whose primary disagreement was over whether the caliph should be a blood descendant of the prophet or if he should be elected. Both strands of the caliphate were eventually retired. For the Sunnis (the sect that believed in elected caliphs), it was formally disbanded in 1922 by the Turkish president who replaced the Sultan of the Ottoman Empire. The Shia (those that thought lineage was necessary) eventually ran out of descendants of the prophet Muhammad and were forced to concede that God had removed the imam (their name for the caliph) from the earth until his return at Armageddon. When al-Baghdadi claimed the mantle of caliph, he was restoring the idea of a worldwide Islamic nation.

With the caliphate restored and in possession of territory for the first time since 1924, ISIS began to propagate its message to the Muslims of the world. Their messaging is based on a detailed narrative that includes their identity, their goals, their enemies, and their end state. That their ranks swelled to more than one hundred thousand followers demonstrates the power and success of that narrative in motivating a diverse base of followers and fighters.

WHO ARE THEY?

Islam is a religion with 1.7 billion adherents around the globe, representing 23 percent of the world's population. These followers are called Muslims. For five hundred years, Islam was the cultural, educational, and scientific center of the world. As the Renaissance dawned in Europe, the influence and relevance of the Islamic capitals waned. Muslims were increasingly pressured to leave Spain and Russia, and the empire began to shrink. Bernard Lewis, a noted Middle East scholar, describes a disastrous attempt to sack Vienna in 1683 as the beginning of the end.[2] The caliphate suffered defeat after defeat, each loss shrinking the empire until it was relegated to modern day Turkey. The caliphate would never recover its former glory. In 1922, Turkish president Mustafa Kemal Ataturk, in an effort to modernize his new country, abolished the Ottoman Sultanate and with it the last remnants of the previously dominant Islamic caliphate.

ISIS and other jihadists claim to be the descendants of those early Muslims who ruled much of the world during Islam's Golden Age from the eighth century to the thirteenth century. They view this period as proof that Islam is both a religion and a successful political system. In the prior caliphate, Muslims, Christians, and Jews lived in relative peace, provided that Christians and Jews acknowledged the dominance of Muslims and paid a regular tax known as the *jizya*.

The jihadists believe that all the world's Muslims owe their allegiance to Islam—and thus, to the Islamic State, too. The modern caliphate is the literal successor of past caliphates. The problem with this line of thought is that from its earliest days there have been disagreements, divisions, and outright wars over the role of Islam in governance and the right of leadership. Different sects of Islam take their guidance from

A member of the Islamic Jihad terror group in Palestine holds up a copy of the Quran during a demonstration in the Gaza Strip. Like ISIS, the Islamic Jihad group seeks to establish a special Islamic state.

differing leaders and scripture, to the point where some sects are identified by the number of the last caliph they consider to be valid. The jihadists themselves represent a tiny portion of a minority interpretation within a particular ideology of only one of the sects of Islam. They are an extreme version of the Wahhabi school of the Salafi mindset of the Sunni sect of Islam.

Jihadist claims of lineage and devoutness justify, in their minds, their legitimacy to claim leadership of the religion and of fellow Muslims. It is this connection to a glorious perceived past that many find so inspiring. Other Muslims who feel disconnected from their current country are told that they belong to a noble tradition of grand warriors who defend the faith and the faithful. If they wish to take their rightful place among their brothers and sisters, they have to come to ISIS-controlled lands and join the fight.

WHAT DO THEY WANT?

The ultimate goal of ISIS is the ushering in of the apocalypse, after which the entire world will be an Islamic State.[3] In this new world, Islamic scripture and tradition will reign supreme. Islamic law, known as Sharia, will be the law of the land. An important part of creating a global Islamic State is the destruction of political borders that separate the world into countries. In one of their first symbolic acts, the group bulldozed a portion of the border between Syria and Iraq and released a video titled "The End of Sykes-Picot."

The title references an agreement between France and Great Britain toward the end of World War I. The two nations drew a line on the map and decided that France would control the territory above the line, and Great Britain would control the lands below. Within these regions, the two world powers created the modern borders of Syria, Iraq, Lebanon, and Jordan, and carved out an international area in Palestine.

JIHADIST IDEOLOGY

From the early days of Islam, there have been those who argued that everything that needed to be known about proper conduct and leadership of Muslims could be known from the Quran, along with the example and sayings of Muhammad and his so-called rightly guided companions. When faced with the splintering and collapse of the caliphate in the modern era, some began to argue that the only way to restore Islam to its former glory was to restore government and behavior to the way everything was before the decline. This idea that the example and wisdom of the ancestors was the model for modern behavior is called Salafism (after the Arabic word for "ancestors"). Wahhabism (named for the preacher who espoused the ideology) developed within this school of thought and began to declare that any innovation beyond the foundations of the religion was sinful. Modern jihadists who subscribe to this ideology have taken this to an even more extreme interpretation. Muslims who had worked toward reconciling their faith with modernity were guilty of crimes against Islam and could be killed as nonbelievers. This was a new and dangerous development that endangers Muslims as much as those of other faiths.

ISIS rejects these modern boundaries and condemns the leaders of these countries as having bowed to Western influence. While these local boundaries are their immediate concern, they also believe that all borders represent an unlawful division of the world's Muslims. The group wants to expand as described in their magazine *Dabiq*, wherein they promise "the shade of the blessed flag will expand until it covers all eastern and western extents of the Earth."[4] The destruction of part of the border between Syria and Iraq, and the establishment of a physical Islamic State, was an important step for the group, but may prove to be their Achilles' heel. If they are driven from their lands and hold no territory, their claims to be a caliphate would be in danger.

If the Islamic faith is to reign supreme over the Earth, ISIS believes it must be purified and restored to its original tenets. Over the last 1,400 years, Islam has undergone a number of changes. ISIS rejects any modernization of the faith. They want

US Representative Michael McCaul (R–Texas) holds up a copy of *Dabiq*, ISIS's propaganda magazine, during a hearing on homeland security in 2014.

TELL ME A TALE

all Muslims to live exactly as Muhammad and his early followers lived. This is bad news for the Shia Muslims who make up nearly 15 percent of the world's Muslims. ISIS considers Shiism to be a forbidden innovation and has killed thousands of Shia in the newly reestablished caliphate.[5] The world's population will be subjected to ISIS's interpretation of Sharia, or Islamic law. Women would be covered and men bearded. Harsh punishment would be meted out to any who fail to adhere to the strict code of religious law.

WHO IS THE ENEMY?

Since ISIS relies on a body of religious texts that is more than a thousand years old, it is sometimes confusing to try to understand who they define as their enemy. They speak often of a great and final battle against the armies of Rome. Adnani, a frequent spokesman, has declared, "We will conquer your Rome, break your crosses, and enslave your women, by the permission of Allah, the Exalted."[6]

While Rome may have been a significant challenger and threat to the early Islamic State, times have changed. In an imaginative leap, ISIS has deemed America the new Rome. Since Europe and other countries around the world have supported American efforts in the Middle East, they have found themselves a target of ISIS's wrath as well. Attacks across Europe have demonstrated ISIS's hatred and disregard for even the civilians of these countries.

Ultimately, any nonbeliever is the enemy. Unfortunately for many Muslims, they find themselves on the list because of their interpretation of their faith or their level of devotion to the terrorists' version of it. Unable to reach its primary enemy, ISIS has contented itself by rounding up and slaughtering those caught in the territories it has seized, with occasional thrusts into the heart of Europe.

WHAT DOES THE FUTURE HOLD?

The reestablishment of the caliphate, despite its detractors, has powerfully centralized the narrative of ISIS. They have clearly detailed the identity to which they lay claim. They use traditional print and modern online media to define this identity while proclaiming their goals and marking their enemies. Their narrative resonates, as shown by the large number of recruits from across the globe who have joined the fight.

Protesters in Palestine demand the reconstitution of the caliphate, or the Islamic State, which was abolished in Palestine nearly a hundred years ago.

The great and final showdown in Dabiq, Syria, that ISIS claims was foretold in prophecy will likely never materialize. The group has lost most of the ground they initially seized and their borders shrink daily. Arab forces, in cooperation with America and other partners, are steadily driving the group from their strongholds. As ISIS loses the land to which it has laid claim, it will be increasingly difficult for the group to claim that it is a caliphate. If they control no land and can dominate no people, then there is little justification for them to continue to call themselves a caliphate.

The danger will survive the loss of a physical caliphate. ISIS will likely shift toward a virtual caliphate. They have established a far-reaching and effective online communication network that will continue to draw recruits to the fold. Their narrative provides a clear story of their identity, goals, enemies, and final state. Without a physical place to go and fight jihad, these new recruits will likely look for opportunities to attack those within reach, leading to a rise in small attacks carried out by isolated individuals or small groups.

In the next chapter we'll explore how ISIS has gone about spreading its message to the world. With production values rivaling movie studios and mainstream print media, their communications are perfectly designed for a modern audience. This messaging remains the primary means of reaching potential recruits outside of ISIS lands and will remain a threat long after the collapse of the physical caliphate. Their efforts are surprisingly sophisticated and involve a complex web of social media, physical outreach, and training. ISIS, the dangerous spider, continues to spin and grow this web to locate and mobilize soldiers dedicated to the story of the group and its dark vision of the future.

3

SPINNING THE WEB

It was four minutes and forty seconds that would shake the world. The video began with a clip of US President Barack Obama announcing airstrikes against ISIS. Then the image shifted. A man dressed in orange, reminiscent of prison clothes, knelt in a vast, empty expanse of desert. Beside him a man dressed all in black, with a mask over his face, stood with a knife. James Foley, the man in orange and an American journalist, began to speak. He spoke to his parents and his brother, saying, "I wish I had more time. I wish I could have the hope for freedom to see my family once again." The man with the knife began to speak English with a British accent, denouncing American actions against ISIS as attacks against all Muslims, a familiar narrative from the group, and promised more bloodshed. The man in black beheaded the young reporter and then the scene shifted. Another man in orange, reporter Steven Sotloff, knelt in front of the camera. The man in black—who would become known as Jihadi John—pointed his knife at the camera menacingly. "The life of this American citizen, Obama, depends on your next decision."[1]

US President Barack Obama makes an announcement about airstrikes against ISIS-held positions in Iraq and Syria in 2014.

JIHAD STUDIOS PRESENTS

The production value of ISIS videos rivals any modern studio. Bright images, steady camera shots, high-definition pictures, and clear sound. But beneath the Hollywood veneer lies a corrupting message that has spread like a cancer, its tendrils reaching across the globe looking for new recruits. The videos are mostly in English, suggesting that they are meant for consumers outside of ISIS lands, where Arabic is the primary language. These are recruitment videos, designed to ensnare Westerners in a tangled web of violence and distorted religious messaging that will excite and enflame the passions of their viewers.

The content of the videos is very diverse. These videos demonstrate an ability to seamlessly edit together a variety of shots and video sources. Shadows on the ground even indicate the usage of studio-style lights and green-screen backgrounds to create the dramatic vistas seen in some of the videos. The graphics in the videos are impressively well designed and executed. They incorporate music and sound files in the form of Quranic recitations and songs, called *nasheeds*. These songs combine modern events with religious messaging and stories about history and are very popular with ISIS and potential recruits.

There are the beheading videos with which we've become all too familiar. Other videos show fighters giving candy, toys, and clothing to children in conquered towns. Some videos show daily life under the caliphate, where bearded men and covered women go about everyday tasks. Those stopped and asked about their life invariably tell of how much better life is under ISIS, but in some you can see the shadow of fear in their eyes. There are videos of battles between ISIS fighters and local as well as international forces, and horrific scenes of bombings and the destruction of cultural artifacts and locations forever lost to history. In several videos, young men sit around in rooms or out in the countryside and talk about their reasons for joining ISIS. The men recite poetry or verses from the Quran and weep as though their level of emotional engagement is somehow indicative of their devotion to the cause. With advancing technology, drone videos are beginning to pop up in the group's media feeds. In a frightening combination of videography and assault, the drone's camera records as the drone releases a mortar shell that falls to the ground, destroying a military vehicle below.

A MEDIA EMPIRE

While the group initially relied on individual postings of blurry videos, snapshots, and other messages on sites like Twitter, YouTube, or other file hosting services, there was no central repository for messages and images. These grainy and disorganized images were inconsistent with how the group viewed itself, so a new media endeavor was born. The messaging needed to be bigger, better, slicker, more violent. As terrorism expert Bruce Hoffman has said, the group has shown its understanding of a potential recruit base "who grew up in a culture of violent movies and video games and are jazzed by it...They are targeting those who see in violence a form of catharsis and a way to strike back at the enemy."[2]

In May 2014, ISIS created the al-Hayat Media Center to manage communications.[3] The center handles all the distribution of images, videos, written messages, audio clips, and even an online magazine. Previously, potential recruits and others looking for ISIS propaganda were dependent on a shaky series of constantly shifting Twitter and Facebook accounts that were subject to banning by these online platforms for violating the terms of service. A network of accounts that was used to spread the messages could be eliminated overnight by a single

HORROR FILMS

The Islamic State didn't invent the idea of the terror video. Years earlier, al-Qaeda, Osama bin Laden's organization and the force behind the September 11, 2001, attacks, released the first beheading video. In May 2004, al-Qaeda released a video titled "Abu Musab al-Zarqawi Slaughters an American." The grainy video shows a group of men beheading an American, Nick Berg, while shouting "*Allahu Akbar,*" or "God is the greatest."

Grainy video clips with poor audio were frequently circulated, but they hardly resonated with the audience ISIS sought to capture. Old men sat around in caves with their weapons perched against the stone walls. Men in dusty clothing fired weapons into an empty desert. These clips were a long way from the slickly produced videos of ISIS, with graphic overlays, high-quality sound, and scenes of actual firefights against the enemy with gruesome ends for those who fell at the hands of ISIS.

With the al-Hayat Media Center, ISIS took their efforts into the modern era. It would serve as a movie studio, publishing house, and public relations firm for the group. Rather than being profit motivated, this movie studio's revenue would be in the flow of new recruits to the cause and the blood of those slain.

complaint from a user of the sites. By centralizing and taking control of their various efforts at messaging, ISIS could now refocus its efforts on recruitment.

Al-Hayat is a powerful new tool that takes the narrative of ISIS and spreads that message across the globe. They paint their members as brave fighters in a global holy war fighting against an evil West that has oppressed and killed Muslims for centuries. According to the propaganda produced by al-Hayat, the fight will end only when they've purified Islam and created a glorious and eternal Islamic State that spans the globe. They spread a message of triumph in battle, of justice for the wronged, of the fairness and stability of their rule over conquered towns, of their righteousness and adherence to a pure version of the faith, and of the responsibility for all to come and join the fight.[4]

A SOCIAL DISEASE

It's been called the cyber caliphate. Dissatisfied with the availability of recruits in locally seized areas, ISIS has reached out across the web to identify and groom those who might come to the fight. Their efforts are a sophisticated blend of social media messaging and smartphone apps that extend the reach of the group. Even as it is losing ground in Iraq and Syria, ISIS's nefarious reach has increased online.

The campaign began the same day that two thousand ISIS soldiers stormed into Mosul, Iraq, driving thirty thousand terrified Iraqi Security Forces before them. It started with the hashtag #AllEyesonISIS. The average age of ISIS fighters is twenty-four years old; they have been raised in the social media era and are more comfortable with Twitter, Facebook, Snapchat, Imgur, Tumblr, Instagram, and other social media platforms than the emails or written letters of bygone eras. These platforms offer an unprecedented opportunity for the terror group to distribute its message or for those seeking information about the group to go in search of that message.[5]

A video released by ISIS in September 2014 shows a masked Islamic State fighter with hostage Steven Sotloff, an American-Israeli journalist, moments before Sotloff was beheaded.

Because websites like Twitter allow for the autonomous spread of trending, or popular, hashtags, ISIS has found a way to reach even those who aren't looking for the sick videos and photos the group distributes. During the 2014 World Cup soccer championship, the hashtag #WorldCup was trending worldwide as the most popular hashtag on Twitter. ISIS began tweeting pictures of a severed head using the hashtag. The result was that anyone following the trending tag found themselves unwittingly viewing terrorist propaganda, with ISIS calling the head their soccer ball.

Young British Muslims came together to denounce ISIS and the terror group's interpretation of the teachings of Islam. Though ISIS claims to speak for all Muslims, few outside of ISIS territory support the group's unique brand of Islam.

THE BLUEPRINT

ISIS's plan to conquer the world is not a random series of acts. In 2004, Abu Musab al-Zarqawi, an al-Qaeda operative and the founder of al-Qaeda in Iraq (AQI), grew tired of the lack of progress in the fight against the West. He knew he needed to inspire a flood of warriors to join the fight in Iraq to defeat the coalition forces there. He bristled against the restrictions his parent group suggested when they cautioned him about attacks on other Muslims. His answer would be a document that continues to guide the Islamic State today.

The Management of Savagery outlines the strategy of AQI. As the group disintegrated and was reformed as the Islamic State in Iraq, and eventually the Islamic State in Iraq and the Sham, this book would be the cornerstone of their strategy. The document calls for fighters to set up in countries with poor governance and to spread from there like evil inkblots until the group covers the entire planet. Part of this strategy involves using our media as a tool against us. Zarqawi knew that the twenty-four-hour news cycle could be exploited to further publicize their activities and messaging.[7] With Western media outlets constantly trying to fill airtime and get page views, it's easy for ISIS to get attention, even for the smallest acts. And as Zarqawi knew, while most of those tuning in are disgusted with what they see, plenty of people learn of ISIS — and find their way to terrorism—because of the constant airplay and the millions of web updates.

Websites like Twitter, Facebook, YouTube, and Google would not sit idly by and let their products be used to spread terror. The companies instituted policies and content filtering that would remove offending accounts while preventing the proliferation of terror messaging. YouTube allows users to report offensive videos, with some users getting a "trusted flagger" status that can immediately remove a video. Other sites use databases of known offensive images to prevent those images from being reposted. Worldwide, governments and private agencies have banded together to combat the messaging of ISIS.[6] Unfortunately, it's a bit like a corrupted game of Whack-a-Mole. Content can be uploaded and spread faster than the companies can keep up. For every image or account or hashtag defeated, more spring up to replace it. It's a difficult fight, but an important one, to protect the world from the poison ISIS would spread.

READ ALL ABOUT IT

In an effort to recruit Western fighters, ISIS has created and distributed an online English-language magazine called *Dabiq*. *Dabiq* is the name of the town in Syria that an ISIS prophecy claims will represent the site of the final battle between the West and Islam and trigger Armageddon. The magazine began in July 2014, combining colorful pictures and modern formatting to tout the group's success in battle, provide religious guidance, instruct readers in terror tactics, and guide recruits on how to avoid detection as they head to Syria or operate in their own countries. One troubling issue even justified the taking and exploitation of sexual slaves from among those conquered by ISIS.[8] The magazine is an important part of ISIS's propaganda machine.

The group has even created smartphone apps that provide information and instructions to followers and would-be recruits. As social media giants step up their enforcement by blocking offensive accounts and message, ISIS has had to go private. The apps they've created collect all the various propaganda into a single access point. They allow access to a dangerous world of messages and images designed to recruit followers and provide lessons on how to carry out attacks. Some hacking groups are exposing and attacking the distributors of these applications in a rare show of cooperation between these groups and the governments with whom they usually tangle.[9]

WELCOME TO THE FOLD

While online methods have brought thousands to the fight, the group continues to use traditional means of recruiting individuals. As borders close  and online messaging is restricted, ISIS has had to branch out to physical recruiting. Leaflets are distributed in ISIS controlled areas that outline the group's philosophy and interpretations

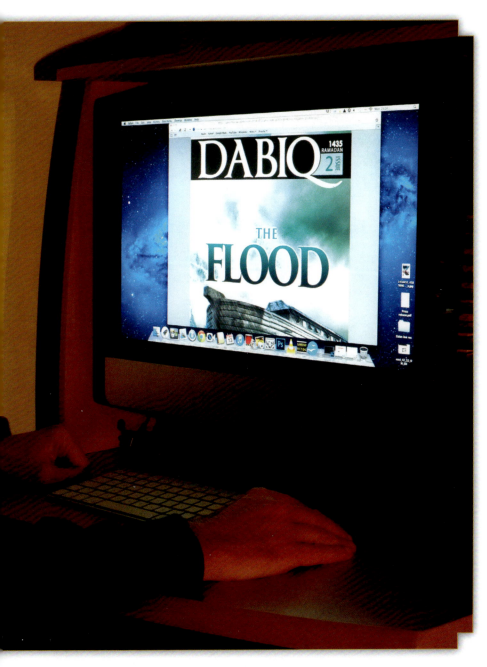

ISIS relies heavily on the internet to recruit members into their fold. They not only use social media, but publish digital copies of their magazine, *Dabiq*, online as well.

Russian law enforcement officials arrest men suspected of recruiting for ISIS and the al-Nusra Front terrorist organization. This phone shows a propaganda video used in recruitment.

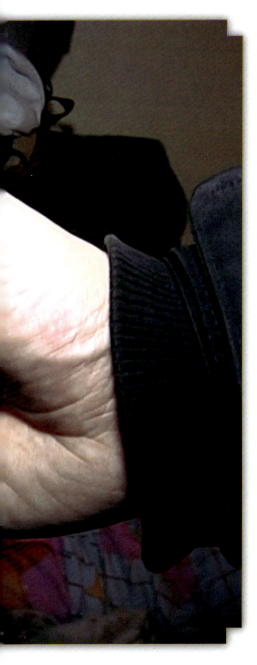

of laws. Some of the group's recruitment occurs with the help of fiery preachers who praise ISIS in their mosques.[10] However, this violent messaging from the pulpits has drawn quick condemnation from many who attend the services. Since most Muslims condemn violent uses of their religion, the preachers who support ISIS often find themselves teaching from the fringes or recruiting new members through smaller study groups.

Online and traditional recruitment messaging has proved extremely effective for the group. In the next chapter, we'll look at how this messaging has spread the group, inspiring affiliates dedicated to the expansion of the Islamic State. Factions of ISIS have been declared in Syria, Afghanistan, Somalia, Nigeria, Libya, the Philippines, and even Australia. These groups represent the growing danger and reach of ISIS as it spreads from the deserts of Iraq and Syria into capitals around the globe, creating an empire of evil that threatens the civilized world.

4

THE SPREADING
DARKNESS

Afghanistan has been called the graveyard of empires after Alexander the Great, Genghis Khan, and the British Empire all ran into troubles in the region.[1] In December 1979, thousands of Soviet troops and tanks would prove the label accurate when they invaded the country and found themselves locked in a decade-long quagmire that would cost billions in lives and treasure, contributing to the collapse of the Soviet Union. After their withdrawal, a group of religious scholars rose to power. They called themselves the Taliban, meaning students, and they would nurse a fledgling group that would shake the world and seek to drive it to Armageddon.

EVIL BORN

Without an enemy, the fighters of the war against the Soviet Union turned their hateful eyes toward a new target. These mujahideen, or holy warriors, settled on the presence of westerners in Muslim lands as the next great enemy. American troops in Saudi Arabia and the ongoing presence of Israel provided the new enemy. A leader, Osama bin Laden, emerged from the fighters and formed a group whose name, al-Qaeda, means "the base" in Arabic. From this "base," a new plan arose. Al-Qaeda would use the permissiveness of the Taliban and the freedom to plan to launch the attacks of September 11, 2001, on New York City's World Trade Center and the Pentagon, outside Washington, DC.

After the United States invaded Afghanistan in 2001, and Iraq a couple of years later, a new affiliate of al-Qaeda sprang up in Iraq under the guidance of a Jordanian jihadist named Abu Musab al-Zarqawi. While originally labeled al-Qaeda in Iraq (AQI), the group would begin to distance itself from their parent group, and instead of expanding slowly, they would

Osama bin Laden, the former leader of al-Qaeda, photographed here in Afghanistan in 2001, helped ISIS get its start. The infamous terror group began as al-Qaeda in Iraq (AQI) in 2004.

execute spectacular attacks to spread their message. These attacks slaughtered Muslims and nonbelievers alike and made no distinction between fighters and innocents.

The declaration of the Islamic State in Iraq and its expansion into Syria was the last straw for al-Qaeda; they distanced themselves from the group in the strongest possible language, declaring that ISIS "is not a branch of the al-Qaeda group ... does not have an organizational relationship with it and [al-Qaeda] is not the group responsible for their actions."[2] Despite losing the support of its parent organization, the seeds for ISIS had taken firm root in the deserts of Iraq and Syria. The holy war would continue in earnest.

TERROR IN THE NAME OF GOD

After a wave of successful attacks and the seizure of Mosul, Iraq, and Raqqa, Syria, the reputation of ISIS rose. Not content with simply being an Islamic State in Iraq and Syria, the group dropped the locations from its name, referring to itself only as the Islamic State, a global caliphate for all Muslims. Under the revised name, ISIS ordered all Muslims to migrate to ISIS lands and all jihadist groups to swear allegiance to the caliphate. Since most jihadist groups were loosely affiliated with al-Qaeda, a new power dynamic evolved. By claiming the caliphate, ISIS established a powerful motivator for other Muslims to join them in defending their lands against modern-day Crusaders and attacking them in their own lands.

While al-Qaeda had always been careful to describe their actions—even the attacks on September 11, 2001—as a defensive jihad, ISIS revels in the offense.[3] Modern jihad can be traced back to an Egyptian scholar, Sayyid Qutb, who used the Quran and Hadith to justify fighting the near enemy in Muslim lands, including foreign forces and even Arab rulers he deemed to be puppets of Western governments. Osama bin Laden turned this jihad outward while still considering these attacks in Western lands as defense against further encroachment. But ISIS has opened the floodgates, attacking not only Western nations, but Muslims who believe differently from their narrow interpretation of Islam.

ISIS promises the reestablishment of a global Muslim community where followers bask in the glory of God's favor and live righteous lives under strict rules. All non-Muslims will defer to their betters in this imagined kingdom. Those who die in the service of the caliphate will be rewarded in heaven with infinite treasures and servants for their every need.

GLORIOUS REWARD

It is difficult to understand why someone would blow themselves up in the name of religion or carry out an attack where they are likely to be killed. One explanation that is frequently suggested is the promise of a reward for martyrs to the cause in the afterlife. Jihadist mythology references a statement by the prophet Muhammad promising seventy-two virgins in heaven as a reward to any martyr.[4] The biggest problem is that none of the references ever actually say anything about virgins.

The word used in most of the references to virgins is *houri*, which has been translated to mean large-eyed women, pure beings, angels, and even white grapes.[5] The Quran mentions these houri several times, but there is no specific number or gender for these heavenly companions. Several scholars have attributed the promise of seventy-two virgins to sayings of the prophet, or Hadith, but there is little agreement on the subject.

ISIS fighters load what they claim are pieces of a crashed US drone into the back of a van in Raqqa, Syria, in 2014, following US-led airstrikes against the group.

The allure of jihad has led to the creation of numerous groups and the rededication of others to ISIS's cause. From seized lands and patrons abroad, the money rolled in, deepening ISIS's influence and expanding their reach to other continents. Oil, hostages, taxes, and foreign donations all brought an unprecedented level of revenue to ISIS, giving it a level of statehood never before seen in jihadist groups. With money came more power, more land, and even more money, in a cycle that lent credibility to the group's claims of the reestablishment of the caliphate.

FOLLOW THE MONEY

In a scene that resembles a video game, black-and-white camera footage shows a scene shot from above. The focus is a nondescript building somewhere in Mosul, Iraq. As the plane overhead circles, the camera shifts to track the building. The black and white picture disappears behind a blinding flash of white as a 2,000-pound (907-kilogram) bomb strikes the house. The picture settles back into black and white, revealing a massive cloud rising from the building. Highlighted against the cloud, thousands of scraps of paper flutter down in the aftermath of the explosion, some of them burning as they twist in the breeze. Millions of dollars were destroyed in the attack, its remnants now coming to rest on the surrounding buildings. The strike was part of a larger effort in which the United States claims to have destroyed $800 million of ISIS's stockpiled cash.[6]

The loss of the cash was a hard blow for ISIS. It pays its fighters and administers social programs in its territory using the funds. Without money, fighters flee and social unrest brews as people whose acceptance of ISIS has been bought with services focus instead on their brutal captors. ISIS estimates its annual expenditures at $2 billion, with a surplus of around $250 million collected through a variety of means.[7] With dwindling cash stores, the group will be hard-pressed to cling to its seized lands.

The group's initial funding came from two primary sources. Wealthy donors from the Persian Gulf provided an estimated $40 million in start-up funds.[8] As the group rolled through Mosul and other towns, ISIS seized money from the local banks and secured control of oil wells and refineries in the newly claimed territories. Before oil prices weakened, ISIS was making $500 million a year from oil sales alone.[9] However, US and coalition airstrikes have been steadily eroding this income source.

In addition to their initial assets, ISIS has raised money through a series of taxes levied against those held in its sway, including an extra tax levied against Christians and Jews. Kidnapping and ransoming hostages has also added to the group's coffers. From high-profile hostages who ransom for millions of dollars to locals who can be ransomed for hundreds or, at best, thousands of dollars, the group has found ways to continue to raise the funds necessary to continue its war and its global expansion, though not at a level that will allow the group to survive continued setbacks.[10]

Smoke billows from a neighborhood in Mosul, Iraq, after Iraqi and allied forces began the fight to retake the city from ISIS in October 2016.

SPREADING THE VIRUS

As the Islamic State grew in infamy, groups around the world offered their *bay'ah*, or pledge of allegiance. While there are no official affiliates in Western Europe or the Americas, the group has managed to expand on nearly every other occupied continent. Some of the groups were previously loyal to al-Qaeda, while others were focused solely on local concerns. Now, they

PLEDGING ALLEGIANCE

One of the pillars of Islam is the *shahada*, or publicly witnessing that there is no god but God. A *bay'ah* is an extension of that public declaration whereby someone declares their loyalty to a leader. When Muhammad swept back into the city of Mecca after his exile to Medina, he required the leaders of all of the local tribes to swear an oath of allegiance to him. While the bay'ah was historically used by those wishing to join the *ummah*, or Islamic nation, it has been used more recently by terror groups in their attempts to establish a hierarchy between groups.

ISIS initially swore a bay'ah to al-Qaeda, but retracted that oath once they began to receive criticism from al-Qaeda over their seizure of Mosul and declaration of an Islamic State.[11] Since the split, the world's terror groups have faced a dilemma: to which group should they pledge allegiance? ISIS now claims that all the world's Muslims have a duty to pledge their loyalty to their leader Baghdadi, since they believe he is the caliph for all Muslims. But since most Muslims refuse to acknowledge ISIS or Baghdadi as anything related to Islam, the majority of Muslims have not and will not swear a bay'ah.

are combining into a cruel network of terror that seeks to strike throughout the globe.

Several groups already close to the caliphate's lands were quick to pledge allegiance. Many of the groups in Syria joined the banner of ISIS, but there are a couple of holdouts, like the Islamic Front and Fatah ash-Sham, that have actually attacked ISIS fighters.[12] Elsewhere in the Middle East, groups have sworn allegiance to ISIS, spreading the group's influence in Yemen, Saudi Arabia, and Egypt. Named for the province in Yemen it calls home, the San'a province of the Islamic State has claimed responsibility for the bombings of several mosques in Yemen. Three Shia mosques in Saudi Arabia have been destroyed by a group calling themselves Najd, after their region in the center of the kingdom. The Sinai Peninsula, which has been largely demilitarized since the early 1970s has seen a surge of activity as Egyptian forces have been battling an ISIS affiliate named for the troubled peninsula. Wilayat Sinai, as the group is known, claimed a string of suicide bombings and the downing of a Russian passenger plane that took off from Sharm ash-Sheikh, a resort on the Red Sea. Hundreds were killed.[13]

Boko Haram in Nigeria, which has pledged allegiance to ISIS, vaulted into the spotlight in April 2014 with the kidnapping of nearly three hundred school girls. The group has been even more vicious than ISIS, killing hundreds more than the group to which it swears allegiance.[14] Groups loyal to ISIS have also formed in Tunisia, Algeria, and Libya, carrying out a few high-profile attacks in the name of the caliphate. Attacks on beach resorts and museums have shaken the tourism industry upon which many depend, creating further chaos and instability.

Other groups have sworn allegiance in the Philippines, Pakistan, and Afghanistan (the heart of al-Qaeda territory). The Caucasus region spawned another group that has carried out

Boko Haram, a Nigerian affiliate of ISIS, frequently kidnaps and holds young African girls. The girls above were rescued by Nigerian military forces in 2015.

attacks in Russia and sent 2,400 soldiers to fight in Syria.[15] The flow of foreign fighters to ISIS lands presents a serious threat. As ISIS loses ground, these fighters will likely return home and seek to wreak havoc locally. While there is no reason to believe ISIS is exercising administrative and operational control over groups from Tunisia all the way to the Philippines, the fighters of these organizations have all pledged their loyalty to the cause and have dedicated themselves to spreading jihad across the globe. Some may have only joined the group for the notoriety and to capitalize on the group's reputation and authority, but others have proved zealous recruits, killing thousands in the name of the caliphate.

In the next chapter, we'll explore what can be done to counter the group and their venomous messaging. It is unlikely that every single terrorist currently fighting in Iraq and Syria, or waging battle on the homefront, will be captured or killed.

Attacking the messaging will require an understanding of the attractiveness of the narrative and a look at other grievances that recruits have reported as motivating factors. The effort is beyond the capability of any government or military to handle alone and will require community engagement and the weight of true scholars of Islam who can counter the messages of jihad and violence. As long as ISIS can broadcast its message, it will continue to find fresh recruits ready to answer the call and commit violence in the name of their twisted version of Islam.

5

TERROR ON THE HOMEFRONT

Mohammad Ibrahim Yazdani was a young engineer living and working in India. At a previous job in Saudi Arabia, a friend of his showed him some ISIS materials from the internet and convinced him that ISIS was doing a good thing. Months later, back home in India, Mohammad tried to reach out to his friend only to discover that his friend had gone to Syria and died for ISIS. Rather than be deterred, Mohammad was inspired. From his Twitter account, he searched for "ISIS" and "caliphate." He quickly found Abu Issa al-Amriki, a Sudanese recruiter and planner for ISIS living deep in Syria. For nearly a year the men spoke frequently as Mohammad tried to find a way into Syria through Greece or Turkey. After repeated failures to get permission to enter even these border countries, al-Amriki suggested another way that Mohammad could serve. If he could not come to jihad, he could bring jihad to those around him.

Mohammad began recruiting others to join his group, and encrypted messages began to direct them to hidden weapons and ammunition with which to carry out the attack. The members of the small group all signed a pledge of allegiance to ISIS and its leader, al-Baghdadi. The time for the big attack was at hand. Mohammad was given directions to a bag of fertilizer and instructions on how to use it to make a lethal killing device. Despite their attempts to follow the steps from a YouTube video, the group was unable to make the explosive correctly. They began discussing their problems on cell phones using the code phrase "cooking the rice." Fortunately, police were listening and decided that the men's problems with "rice" were probably not culinary in nature. The police raided the home and found the goopy mess that was meant to be a terrifying explosive and arrested the men. Al-Amriki, the plot's mastermind, who had coordinated dozens of other attacks around the globe, thought himself safe in Syria. In April 2016, American forces tracked the recruiter to a neighborhood in al-Bab, Syria, and dropped a bomb onto his apartment, killing him instantly.[1]

HOMECOMING

The Central Intelligence Agency (CIA) estimates that thirty thousand fighters have come from around the world to fight for ISIS in Iraq and Syria.[2] While many will die in the harsh desert, some of them will come home. ISIS-directed attacks have occurred from Indonesia to France, while ISIS-inspired attacks have spanned the globe. The threat of fighters returning to wage war on their home turf has left security officials scrambling to identify those who have left and apprehend them upon their return. With most fighters entering Iraq and Syria from surrounding countries, creating a list of potential threats is not as easy as it would initially seem.

The United Kingdom has reached out to local communities where ISIS fighters have emigrated from to identify others who are trying to join the fight. The lack of trust between security forces and the communities that frequently bear the brunt of their efforts has been a stumbling block. Parents who want to report their kids to keep them safe are faced with the prospect of finding their child in jail instead of Syria or Iraq. The United Kingdom has taken steps to remove the stigma from their processes by partnering with local mosques and groups like the Quilliam Foundation, founded by a former radical who can speak directly to the dangers of jihadist ideology.[3]

A Palestinian Salafist protests against the cartoon images of the Prophet Muhammad printed in the French satirical magazine *Charlie Hebdo* in January 2015.

Arab countries that have strong intelligence and police agencies have leveraged a system of neighborhood agents called *muqadams*. These agents know the names of every individual in their neighborhood and can quickly identify those who go missing so that authorities can be on the lookout for their return. While such measures are impractical in the West, providing alternate pathways for communities and families to seek help with a radicalizing member offers a powerful tool to help potential terrorists before they become further radicalized. Even if only 10 percent of those who have gone to fight return home, there would be approximately three thousand war-hardened, radicalized jihadists looking for ways to bring the war home to their countries of origin.

SPANNING THE GLOBE

The *New York Times* reports that, since 2014, more than 1,200 people have been killed outside of Iraq and Syria at the hands of terrorists directed or inspired by ISIS. While the largest attack was in Egypt with the downing of a Russian passenger plane, nearly half of those killed have been Westerners.[4] Attacks in Paris and Brussels killed 160 and wounded hundreds and were quickly claimed by the terrorist group. These reports don't include those killed in attacks by the original parent group of ISIS, al-Qaeda.

The global reach of ISIS between ordered and inspired attacks demonstrates that the threat is not limited to the harsh lands of Iraq and Syria. While the group has been unable to organize massive attacks on the scale of 9/11, it has made its aims clear. A chilling recording from ISIS tells would-be recruits that "If you are not able to find an IED or a bullet, then single out the disbelieving American, Frenchman, or any of their allies. Smash his head with a rock, or slaughter him with a knife,

CIVIL WAR

It is tempting to lump extremist groups into a single entity, but their differences have led to conflict within and between the groups. Even though ISIS was originally part of al-Qaeda, their relationship has been fraught with peril. While al-Qaeda is comfortable killing those it deems infidels, ISIS has thrown al-Qaeda's rulebook out the window and carried out massive attacks against other Muslims. ISIS believes modernists—and even Shia, who believe in an alternate lineage of leaders from Sunnis—are guilty of innovation and polytheism.

Stranger still were al-Qaeda's attempts to disown ISIS for its extreme violence. The group that carried out the September 11, 2001, attacks and other atrocities around the globe has called ISIS too violent and too indiscriminate in its targeting. ISIS has proved happy to shed its lecturing parent organization and has even clashed with al-Qaeda fighters in Syria.

or run him over with your car, or throw him down from a high place, or choke him, or poison him."[5] This and other messages have inspired attacks around the globe, even from individuals who have not travelled to Iraq or Syria.

The only reliable way to prevent those who have travelled abroad to join ISIS in fighting for the Islamic State at home is to identify those who have left in the first place. The flood of refugees from the war-torn region has made it incredibly difficult for European authorities to separate the innocents from the killers among them. The lack of reliable identification paperwork compounds the issue. The threat from returning fighters is compounded by those who are directed through

Mourners gather outside a market in Paris, France, to pay their respects to those killed in terror attacks in the City of Lights in January 2015. ISIS would later accept the blame for the attacks in Paris.

LONE WOLF

The term "lone wolf" comes from a troubling source. The term was originally used by white supremacist groups to describe individuals who were "warriors acting alone or in small groups who attacked the government or other targets in daily, anonymous acts."[6] Brian Michael Jenkins from the Rand Corporation hates the term. It sounds too cool, too lethal. Instead, he likes to refer to these individuals as stray dogs, because they "skulk about, sniffing at violence, vocally aggressive but skittish without backup."[7]

This type of attack is not unique to jihadist terrorism. The Oklahoma City bombing in 1995 was carried out by a Catholic man who had a grievance against the US government. Regardless of their motivations, these types of attacks are difficult to stop because an individual or small group can largely operate without drawing attention—until they spring their attack. While mental illness has been identified as a factor in some attacks, many of the perpetrators have been frighteningly sane.[8]

online communications to carry out attacks. Programs around the globe have sought to identify these individuals and their paths to radicalization in an effort to stem the flood of fighters to the conflicts in Iraq and Syria—and try to prevent homegrown terror attacks as well.

LONE WOLVES

While no ISIS-organized attacks have been carried out in America, men and women inspired by the jihadist group have killed innocents in the name of ISIS. These attackers represent a relatively unique threat and have been called "lone wolves." The lone wolf is a single attacker, or a small group, who carries out attacks motivated by some ideology or group, but is not directly ordered to action by a member of the larger organization. While counterterrorism officials have been largely successful at thwarting organized attacks, these lone wolves can slip through the cracks—to deadly consequence.

Rizwan Farook and his wife, Tashfeen Malik, left their six-month-old baby girl with her grandmother and headed out to a holiday party hosted by the company Farook worked for. Their clothes seemed a bit strange for a holiday party; the two were dressed in black tactical gear common among police and the military. Farook carried a large bag. Before entering the party, the two smashed their cell phones and tossed them into a garbage can. As they entered the building, the two withdrew two rifles and two pistols from the bag, leaving a remote-controlled car strapped with explosives securely in the bag. They shot and killed fourteen people, and after a short chase, died themselves as twenty-one officers opened fire on the couple. The investigation later revealed additional explosives at the couple's home and a Facebook post declaring their loyalty to the leader of ISIS.[9]

Elton Simpson had been on the FBI's radar since a 2006 attempt to go to Somalia and fight with jihadists there. After Simpson retweeted a message calling for attacks on a contest featuring cartoons of the Muslim prophet Muhammad (depictions of the prophet are forbidden in Islam), the FBI sent a picture of Simpson and warned local police to be on the lookout. Security for the event was already high because there was concern that the event could attract violence. When Simpson and his roommate pulled up to the event and opened fire with

Police and firefighters in San Bernadino, California, cordon off an area after a couple claiming allegiance to ISIS staged a mass shooting at an office holiday party. Fourteen people were killed and twenty-two injured.

assault rifles, they were killed by an off-duty cop who had been hired as security for the event.[10]

NO PLACE TO GO

The little girl and her family were trapped. She was ten years old. Her family had fled after their town descended into the madness of a regional war. They managed to make it to a neighboring country, where her father tried to leverage what little influence and money he could muster to get permission to enter the United States. The family's application was buried in a stack of three hundred thousand others. Three long years passed. Unable to return home and forbidden to move forward, the family languished in limbo. The girl's mother was captured and sent to a labor camp; her last present to her daughter was a diary. The little girl was able to escape capture by hiding with the remnants of her family for a while, but eventually she was captured and killed. You might have read her diary. Her name was Anne Frank and the year was 1942.[11]

The refugees of today would recognize the struggles of refugees throughout history. The conflicts in Syria, Iraq, and Yemen have displaced twenty-three million people.[12] Many of

Forced to flee their homes because of fighting between ISIS and Iraqi forces, citizens of Mosul take up residence in refugee camps like the Hamman al-Alil camp south of Mosul.

them are scattered in camps at the borders of neighboring countries, desperate for a new life. Those who can afford to pay smugglers set off across the treacherous desert or pile into boats that frequently capsize under the excessive weight. Dead children have washed up on the shores of Europe's pristine beaches. Most refugees have no paperwork to prove their identity. Some among them have nefarious purposes and have used the refugee story to sneak into Europe and carry out attacks.[13]

It is a terrible and difficult puzzle with no easy solution. The world mourns the plight of the refugees while trembling in fear at the threat of more attacks. It is exactly as ISIS wants. The more Muslim suffering and death they can blame on the West, the more they can push their message that this is a war between Muslims and the West. They ignore that the millions who have fled are mostly trying to escape from the chaos sown by their brutally violent regime.

In the next chapter we'll look at how the world is trying to combat the global recruitment of ISIS. From interrupting the message to destroying the messenger, the world's attention is on ISIS. The human toll has been steep and will continue to worsen unless the flow of fighters can be stopped and ISIS smothered in its desert hearth. With the flames of ISIS extinguished, the world can turn its focus to undoing the harm that has been wrought in the region.

DRAINING THE SWAMP

Four young men sat with their lawyer in front of a judge, facing a sentence of fifteen years each. Their crime: providing support to ISIS. The men, some of them still teens, had been apprehended while trying to join the fight in Syria and Iraq. Michael Davis, the judge in the case, surprised everyone by ordering a study by a deradicalization expert to determine whether the men could be rehabilitated instead of jailed. The judge said, "It does not make sense why someone who's never been involved in any type of criminal activity, was not seriously religious, [would] in a very short period of time want to go over and be involved in jihad."[1] It was a bold move in the effort to combat the recruitment efforts of ISIS.

BREAKING THE CHAIN

Initial efforts by law enforcement agencies to understand the radicalization process have likened it to a conveyor belt or an escalator that moves a previously nonviolent individual to action.[2] The New York Police Department detailed a four-step

US District Judge Michael Davis, of Minnesota, has tried multiple Americans for attempting to provide support to ISIS or flee to ISIS-held territory.

process of radicalization: pre-radicalization, self-identification, indoctrination, and jihadization. By their logic, an ordinary individual with some grievance could come to identify with a radical group, then be groomed by that group toward further radicalization until the individual commits to violence in support of the group's goals.

Critics of this metaphor have pointed to the lack of a common path for jihadists. They come from all backgrounds and find jihad by a multitude of paths. Not everyone with a grievance will be motivated to join a group of like-minded individuals. Similarly, not every member of a group would be willing to enact violence against others. Despite their disagreements over the exact path to radicalization, most scholars agree that it is a process.[3] A vulnerable individual must first commit to an ideology that encourages violence against the perceived enemies of that ideology before becoming violent themselves.

Fortunately, there are off-ramps that are either self-imposed or systemically enforced. However, we need a better understanding of the process to prevent individuals from beginning their journey to radicalization, interrupt those already on the path, and rehabilitate those who have fallen under the sway of radical groups, if possible. The difficulty of finding solutions stems from the variance in the process. A program that works for some individuals may be totally useless for those who have been motivated or indoctrinated by different methodologies.

If we accept that radicalization is a process that stems from a grievance, then efforts are necessary to alleviate the sources of grievance, attack the sources and means of information, and weaken the narrative that terrorists use to draw recruits into the fold. A process can be interrupted if it is understood well enough, but the messenger is incredibly important. An angry teenager struggling with alienation, looking for a meaningful identity and significance to his life is not likely to be dissuaded from tone-deaf tweets from government agencies.

COMMUNITY OUTREACH

The most effective answer to the challenge might be found right here at home. Peter Neumann, the director of the International Center for the Study of Radicalization and Political Violence in London, offers four suggestions for creating community-based solutions to the problem: messaging, engagement and outreach, capacity-building, and education and training.[4] His ideas have been put to the test around the world, from Saudi Arabia, to England, to the United States, though it is tricky to conduct a counter-radicalization or deradicalization program without unduly focusing on Muslims, since Islamic terror is the target of most of these programs.

The New York Police Department (NYPD) faced a particular challenge with its community outreach program. They needed to offer a program that could be separated enough from policing and intelligence gathering to have credibility with the community and individuals. To solve the problem, the NYPD created a separated Community Affairs Bureau within the department. The program has branches that deal with clergy and immigrant outreach programs in an effort to attack the problem from

Russian security forces detain multiple men accused of recruiting for ISIS and al-Nusra Front in St. Petersburg. Both groups have been banned in Russia.

multiple angles. It is difficult to say if the program has been effective as there is no way to reliably measure outcomes within the program.[6]

The United Kingdom created a similar counter-radicalization program called PREVENT. The program seeks to solve the problem by supporting moderate Islamic leaders, preventing radicalization, increasing community resilience,

Following an attack in Nice, France, claimed by ISIS, officers of the New York City Police Department increased patrols around Times Square and other popular New York destinations.

reducing discrimination, and mentoring vulnerable individuals. The program suffers from some of the same problems as other programs in that it has been accused of focusing only on Muslims. The strength of the program relies on the level of community engagement, which can help resolve issues before

they become crises. By partnering with local, moderate organizations, the United Kingdom has found inroads to vulnerable populations without harsh government interference.[7]

Saudi Arabia, meanwhile, claims an 80 percent success rate in reforming 3,033 radicals, but those numbers are difficult to independently verify.[8] The country is in a unique position as a major mouthpiece for Islamic ideology, with impressive financial resources to address the problem. Their program reeducates participants in the true tenets of Islam while providing an impressive social support network that includes jobs, cars, and houses for graduates of the program. The success of the program highlights the importance of reeducating individuals who have accepted a twisted version of the faith in justifying their actions.

GOING ON THE OFFENSE

"Just like we dropped bombs, we're dropping cyber bombs," announced Ashton Carter, then the deputy US secretary of defense.[9] For the military, cyber warfare is just one more front in a battle that has included land, sea, air, and space elements to combat ISIS. From beaconing programs that map networks, to targeted hacks of devices supporting command and control or messaging, to offensive measures to physically or virtually

Former US secretary of defense Ashton Carter greets Massud Barzani, the leader of Iraqi Kurdistan, in 2016. Iraqi Kurds have been on the frontline of the fight against ISIS since the terrorist group's founding.

HUG A TERRORIST

Denmark is known for its colorful buildings and streets full of bicycles, but it is gaining renown for a very unique approach to counterterrorism. While many European countries are cracking down on mosques or revoking the passports of those suspected of fighting abroad, Aarhus, the second-largest city in Denmark, has worked to reintegrate returning fighters with a message of love and community. The program also helps those who are considering joining terror groups by providing counseling, education, and employment opportunities in an effort to deradicalize these individuals before they become a danger to themselves or others.

Since failure to integrate and anger are primary motivators, the so-called Aarhus method works to alleviate these motivators and find ways for meaningful engagement. The program also allows authorities to monitor these individuals without resorting to harsh crackdowns or discriminatory practices that could further inflame tensions. By approaching these individuals with love, forgiveness, and acceptance, Aarhus has cut the number of its citizens going to fight jihad from twenty-five in 2012 to only one in 2015. Hundreds of other potential recruits have also received services from the program and decided not to fight.[5]

destroy these threats, the military has been exploring new tools in the fight against ISIS.

Social media companies have launched their own efforts to disrupt and suppress the violent images, videos, and messages of ISIS. Twitter actively deletes offensive tweets and bans the accounts that create or spread these messages. It's a murky question as to whether such efforts violate free speech, rob us of intelligence sources, or actually impact the terrorist networks.[11] The US government recently convened a meeting with almost fifty different social media companies, community groups, and government agencies to explore solutions to the problem of ISIS propaganda.[12]

Aside from the virtual efforts to diminish the global recruiting of ISIS, there are some very physical operations designed to destroy the group, or at least its affiliates. In Iraq and Syria, a coalition of Middle Eastern and Western militaries is relying on air power to reclaim territory claimed by ISIS. Boko Haram, the ISIS affiliate in Nigeria, has found itself besieged on all sides by the militaries of surrounding countries. The effectiveness of such efforts is best indicated by the lack of centrally organized attacks on Western nations, leaving ISIS to rely on lone-wolf actors to carry out attacks.

RECLAIMING THE FAITH

The message of ISIS is clearly a powerful motivating force. It claims to be the purest representation of the Islamic faith, which it says is under siege from all sides. There is a very mathematical problem with their claim. Estimates of the group's numbers have put them at anywhere from twenty thousand to two hundred thousand fighters.[13] That means that, at the highest estimate, ISIS represents approximately .01 percent of Muslims. They are outnumbered 8,500 to 1 by Muslims who mostly view the group

Palestinian Christian and Muslim clergymen join forces to show support for those attacked by ISIS after two churches in Egypt were bombed by ISIS and dozens of Christian worshipers were killed in 2016.

unfavorably.[14] This disparity demonstrates a powerful opportunity to counter ISIS's assertion that they represent Islam.

ISIS twists and perverts the scriptures of Islam to justify its bloody campaign for world domination. Muslim leaders and scholars have tried repeatedly to counter the message of ISIS by pointing out all the flaws, misinterpretations, and outright falsehoods in the group's beliefs.[15] Governments have tried to amplify this message but have followed an unclear strategy to identify so-called moderate Muslims. Use of the term "moderate" is fraught with peril, as only Muslims can decide who represents their core message, and there are multiple disagreements and significant divides within the faith. Regardless, no group can be universally held suspect because of the actions of such a small minority of violent radicals.

THE WAY FORWARD

In a short period of time, ISIS has risen from the ashes of al-Qaeda's ill-fated operation in Iraq and seized the attention of the world. Not content with its span of desert control, ISIS has spread its web to every corner of the world as it attempts to lure new recruits and inspire attacks. As military successes against the group continue, it will find itself increasingly in peril, but destroying the head and heart of ISIS will not completely remove the threat. The narrative to which the group ascribes has been inspiring and motivating violence for nearly one hundred years. It cannot be defeated with bombs or guns.

The effort to root out the weeds of ISIS will require global and cultural cooperation on a scale never before seen. ISIS does not recognize the world's boundaries, but it is those very divisions that have helped provide the group space to take root and grow. Countering global recruitment requires a global community that upholds universal human rights. Religion is an

STUXNET

It was supposed to be an impenetrable network. The computers that ran the centrifuges for Iran's nuclear program were not connected to any external network. But after secreting bits of code on computers sold to the Iranians, America was able to map the clandestine efforts at enrichment. The way in turned out to be simple: thumb drives. When workers inserted the drives into the computers, essentially defeating the air gap between the closed network and the internet, a snippet of code known as a worm was uploaded.

Once in place, the worm, later dubbed Stuxnet, would lay dormant. Seemingly at random, the worm would awaken and interfere with the centrifuges as they spun faster than the speed of sound. The result was the destruction of nearly a fifth of Iran's centrifuges. Everything went according to plan—until the worm escaped the closed Iranian network and began to infect computers around the globe.[10] The jig was up, but the worm had accomplished its mission. With the level of interconnectedness in the modern world, the existence of cyber weapons like Stuxnet adds a dimension to future conflicts that could cause problems on a massive scale. Viruses and worms could prove to be the nuclear weapons of the future.

Now, with the knowledge and success of Stuxnet, agencies fighting ISIS are looking at ways to use similar worms in their attacks on the leaders of the terrorist group. If a simple snippet of code can bring down the Iranian centrifuge network, many believe that it should be even easier to tackle ISIS's cyber network—if they can keep the network visible long enough to insert the worm.

important part of life for many people, but those beliefs cannot be allowed to divide the people of the world into camps of us versus them.

ISIS tells recruits that they are in an apocalyptic battle against a world that seeks to stamp out their faith. They are told that they can wage honorable jihad in the service of the Islamic State, that a glorious reward awaits in the afterlife if they kill and die in God's name. These promises must be revealed for the lies they are. In our interconnected world that communicates at the speed of light, our message must be clear: the world and all its people reject ISIS and its message of terror and fear. Our love and respect for one another is stronger than the hate ISIS would use to divide us.

CHAPTER NOTES

Chapter 1: Come to Jihad

1. Scott Bronstein and Drew Griffin. "Young ISIS recruit: I was blinded by love," CNN, December 2, 2016. http://www.cnn.com/2016/12/02/us/mississippi-isis-muhammad-dakhlalla-interview.
2. Rukmini Callimachi. "ISIS and the Lonely American," *New York Times*, June 27, 2015. https://www.nytimes.com/2015/06/28/world/americas/isis-online-recruiting-american.html?_r=0.
3. Matt Bradley. "Rift Grows in Islamic State between foreign, local fighters," *Wall Street Journal*, March 25, 2016. https://www.wsj.com/articles/rift-grows-in-islamic-state-between-foreign-local-fighters-1458930063.
4. Martha Crenshaw. "The Causes of Terrorism," *Comparative Politics*, Vol. 13, No. 4. (Jul., 1981), pp. 379-399 (quote from p 390).
5. Ahmed Al-Dawoody (2011). *The Islamic Law of War: Justifications and Regulations*. Palgrave Macmillan. p. 56.
6. Peter R. Neumann. "Foreign Fighter total in Syria/Iraq now exceeds 20,000; surpasses Afghanistan conflict in the 1980s," ICSR Department of War Studies, King's College London. http://icsr.info/2015/01/foreign-fighter-total-syriairaq-now-exceeds-20000-surpasses-afghanistanconflict-1980s.
7. Claire Healy. "Targeting Vulnerabilities: The Impact of the Syrian War and Refugee Situation on Trafficking in Persons, a Study of Syria, Turkey, Lebanon, Jordan and Iraq," International Centre for Migration Policy Development. http://www.icmpd.org/fileadmin/ICMPD-Website/ICMPD_General/Publications/2016/Targeting_Vulnerabilities_EN__SOFT_.pdf.
8. Carolyn Hoyle, Alexandra Bradford, and Ross Frenett. "Becoming Mulan: Female Western Migrants to ISIS," Institute for Strategic Dialogue, 2015. http://www.strategicdialogue.org/wp-content/uploads/2016/02/ISDJ2969_Becoming_Mulan_01.15_WEB.pdf, p. 11-14.
9. Karen D. Keyes-Turner. "The Violent Islamic Radicalization Process: A Framework for Understanding," Master's thesis, Naval Postgraduate School, 2011. http://www.dtic.mil/dtic/tr/fulltext/u2/a556429.pdf.

10. Peter Neumann."What Motives and Circumstances Lie Behind Persons Affiliating with Violent, Radical-Islamist Groups and Committing Acts of Violence Themselves?" (lecture at the autumn conference of the German Bundeskriminalamt, or Federal Criminal Police Office, Wiesbaden, Germany, Oct 19, 2010).
11. Randy Borum."Understanding Terrorist Psychology," in Andrew Silke, ed. *The Psychology of Counter-Terrorism*. Oxon, UK.: Routledge, 2010.
12. "Austrian ISIS 'Poster Girl' Reportedly Beaten to Death After Trying to Escape Syria," Fox News, November 25, 2015. http://www.foxnews.com/world/2015/11/25/austrian-isis-poster-girl-reportedly-murdered-after-trying-to-escape-syria.html.

Chapter 2: Tell Me a Tale

1. Joby Warrick. *Black Flags: The Rise of ISIS*. New York, NY: Anchor Books, 2016, 633-4.
2. Bernard Lewis. "The Revolt of Islam," *New Yorker*, November 19, 2001. http://www.newyorker.com/magazine/2001/11/19/the-revolt-of-islam.
3. Graeme Wood. "What ISIS Really Wants," *Atlantic*, March 2015. https://www.theatlantic.com/magazine/archive/2015/03/what-isis-really-wants/384980/.
4. Tim Lister. "What Does ISIS Really Want," CNN, December 11, 2015. http://www.cnn.com/2015/12/11/middleeast/isis-syria-iraq-caliphate/.
5. Aryn Baker. "ISIS Claims Massacre of 1700 Iraqi Soldiers," *Time*, June 15, 2014. http://time.com/2878718/isis-claims-massacre-of-1700-iraqis/.
6. Caleb Weiss. "Islamic State Spokesman Again Threatens West in New Speech," Threat Matrix (blog), Long War Journal, September 21, 2014. http://www.longwarjournal.org/archives/2014/09/islamic_state_spokesman_again.php.

Chapter 3: Spinning the Web

1. Jihadist News. "IS Beheads Captured American James Wright Foley, Threatens to Execute Steven Joel Sotloff," Site Intel Group, August 19, 2014. https://news.siteintelgroup.com/jihadist-News/is-beheads-captured-american-james-foley-threatens-to-execute-another.html.

2. Jeffrey Fleishman. "Islamic State and its increasingly sophisticated cinema of terror," *LA Times*, February 26, 2015. http://www.latimes.com/entertainment/movies/la-et-mn-ca-isis-video-horror-20150301-story.html.
3. Olivia Becker. "ISIS Has a Really Slick and Sophisticated Media Department," Vice News. https://news.vice.com/article/isis-has-a-really-slick-and-sophisticated-media-department.
4. Lawrence A. Husick. "The Islamic State's Electronic Outreach," E-Notes, Foreign Policy Research Institute, September 2014. http://www.fpri.org/docs/husick_-_media_war_1.pdf.
5. P. W. Singer and Emerson Brooking. "Terror on Twitter," *Popular Science*, December 11, 2015. http://www.popsci.com/terror-on-twitter-how-isis-is-taking-war-to-social-media.
6. Joseph Menn. "Facebook, Google, and Twitter are stepping up the fight against Islamic extremism online—but they're keeping it quiet," *Business Insider*, December 6, 2015. http://www.businessinsider.com/r-social-media-companies-step-up-battle-against-militant-propaganda-2015-12?r=UK&IR=T&dom=psc&loc=contentwell&lnk=twitters-recent-ban.
7. Brendan I. Koerner. "Why ISIS is Winning the Social Media War," *WIRED*, April 2016. https://www.wired.com/2016/03/isis-winning-social-media-war-heres-beat/.
8. David Denby. "The Perfect Children of ISIS: Lessons from Dabiq," *New Yorker*, November 24, 2015. http://www.newyorker.com/culture/cultural-comment/the-perfect-children-of-isis-lessons-from-dabiq.
9. Don Reisinger. "ISIS has a New Weapon: A Smartphone App," *Forbes*, December 10, 2015. http://fortune.com/2015/12/10/isis-smartphone-app/.
10. Shiv Malik and Sandra Laville. "Isis Recruitment Moves from Online Networks to British Mosques," *Guardian*, September 5, 2014. https://www.theguardian.com/world/2014/sep/05/isis-recruitment-moves-to-radical-network-and-mosques.

Chapter 4: The Spreading Darkness

1. Milton Bearden. "Afghanistan, Graveyard of Empires," *Foreign Affairs*, November 1, 2001. https://www.foreignaffairs.com/articles/afghanistan/2001-11-01/afghanistan-graveyard-empires.

2. Liz Sly. "Al-Qaeda Disavows any Ties with Radical Islamist ISIS group in Syria, Iraq" *Washington Post*, February 3, 2014. https://www.washingtonpost.com/world/middle_east/al-qaeda-disavows-any-ties-with-radical-islamist-isis-group-in-syria-iraq/2014/02/03/2c9afc3a-8cef-11e3-98ab-fe5228217bd1_story.html?utm_term=.11cc16b0b143
3. Fawaz Gerges, "Islamic State: Can its Savagery be Explained?" BBC news, September 9, 2014. http://www.bbc.com/news/world-middle-east-29123528.
4. Abu `Isa Muhammad ibn `Isa at-Tirmidhi, "Regarding the Rewards for the Martyr," The Book on the Virtues of Jihad, Sunnah.com. https://sunnah.com/tirmidhi/22/46.
5. Berg, Herbert (1999). "Ibn Warraq (ed): The Origins of the Koran: Classic Essays on Islam's Holy Book". Bulletin of the School of Oriental and African Studies. 62 (3): 557–558.
6. "Islamic State: Up to $800m of funds 'destroyed by strikes'," BBC News, April 26, 2016. http://www.bbc.com/news/world-middle-east-36145301.
7. Jose Pagliary. "Inside the $2 Billion ISIS War Machine," CNN.com, December 11, 2015. http://money.cnn.com/2015/12/06/news/isis-funding/.
8. Elizabeth Dickinson. "Why Private Gulf Financing for Syria's Extremist Rebels Risks Igniting Sectarian Conflict at Home," Brookings Institution, February 28, 2016. https://www.brookings.edu/wp-content/uploads/2016/06/private-gulf-financing-syria-extremist-rebels-sectarian-conflict-dickinson.pdf
9. Pagliary, "Inside the $2 Billion."
10. Stanford University. "The Islamic State," Mapping Militant Organizations, April 4, 2016. http://web.stanford.edu/group/mappingmilitants/cgi-bin/groups/view/1.
11. J. M. Berger. "The Islamic State vs. al Qaeda," *Foreign Policy*, September 2, 2014. http://foreignpolicy.com/2014/09/02/the-islamic-state-vs-al-qaeda/.
12. Stanford University. "Global Islamic State," Mapping Militants. Accessed March 6, 2017. http://web.stanford.edu/group/mappingmilitants/cgi-bin/maps/view/islamic-state.
13. Karen Leigh, Jason French, and Jovi Juan. "Islamic State and Its Affiliates," *Wall Street Journal*, April 2016. http://graphics.wsj.com/islamic-state-and-its-affiliates/.

14. Priyanka Boghani. "Where the Black Flag Flies," Frontline, May 13, 2016. http://apps.frontline.org/isis-affiliates/
15. Lee et al., "Where the Black Flag," WSJ.

Chapter 5: Terror on the Homefront

1. Rukmini Callimachi. "Not 'Lone Wolves' After All: How ISIS Guides World's Terror Plots from Afar," *New York Times*, February 4, 2017. https://www.nytimes.com/2017/02/04/world/asia/isis-messaging-app-terror-plot.html?_r=0.
2. Eric Schmitt and Somini Engupta. "Thousands Enter Syria to Join ISIS Despite Global Efforts," *New York Times*, September 26, 2015. https://www.nytimes.com/2015/09/27/world/middleeast/thousands-enter-syria-to-join-isis-despite-global-efforts.html?_r=0.
3. Kris Chrismann. "Preventing Religious Radicalisation and Violent Extremism: A Systematic Review of the Research Evidence." Youth Justice Board, 2012. https://www.gov.uk/government/uploads/system/uploads/attachment_data/file/396030/preventing-violent-extremism-systematic-review.pdf.
4. Karen Yourish, Derek Watkins, Tom Giratikanon, and Jasmine C. Lee. "How Many People Have Been Killed in ISIS Attacks Around the World," *New York Times*, July 16, 2016. https://www.nytimes.com/interactive/2016/03/25/world/map-isis-attacks-around-the-world.html.
5. Sophie Inge. "ISIS Orders Killing of 'Spiteful, Dirty' French," Local, September 22, 2014. https://www.thelocal.fr/20140922/isis-urges-killing-of-spiteful-and-dirty-french.
6. Kimmel, Michael, *Angry White Men: American Masculinity at the End of an Era* (Avalon, New York, 2013), pp. 228–9.
7. Brian Michael Jenkins. "Stray Dogs and Virtual Armies: Radicalization and Recruitment to jihadist Terrorism in the United States Since 9/11," Rand Corporation, 2011. http://www.rand.org/content/dam/rand/pubs/occasional_papers/2011/RAND_OP343.pdf.
8. Lydia Alfaro-Gonzalez et al."Report: Lone Wolf Terrorism," Georgetown Security Studies Review, June 27, 2015. http://georgetownsecuritystudiesreview.org/wp-content/uploads/2015/08/NCITF-Final-Paper.pdf

9. Saeed Ahmed. "Who were Syd Rizwan Farook and Tashfeen Malik?" CNN, December 4, 2015. http://www.cnn.com/2015/12/03/us/syed-farook-tashfeen-malik-mass-shooting-profile/.
10. Adam Goldman and Mark Berman, "FBI Had Known About Suspected Terrorist for Years," *Washington Post*, May 4, 2015. https://www.washingtonpost.com/news/post-nation/wp/2015/05/04/fbi-had-known-about-suspected-texas-shooter-for-years/?utm_term=.4353e3886286
11. Elahe Izadi, "Anne Frank and Her Family Were Also Denied Entry as Refugees to the U.S.," *Washington Post*, November 24, 2105. https://www.washingtonpost.com/news/worldviews/wp/2015/11/24/anne-frank-and-her-family-were-also-denied-entry-as-refugees-to-the-u-s/
12. Phillip Connor. "Middle East's Migrant Population More than Doubles since 2005," Pew Research Center, October 18, 2016. http://www.pewglobal.org/2016/10/18/conflicts-in-syria-iraq-and-yemen-lead-to-millions-of-displaced-migrants-in-the-middle-east-since-2005/.
13. Marco Funk and Roderick Parkes. "Refugees vs Terrorists," European Institute for Security Studies, January 2016. http://www.iss.europa.eu/uploads/media/Alert_6_Refugees_versus_terrorists.pdf.

Chapter 6: Draining the Swamp

1. Stephen Montemayor and Mila Koumpilova. "Terror Suspects Will Test Deradicalization Program," *Star Tribune*, March 2, 2016. http://www.startribune.com/judge-orders-de-radicalization-study-for-4-terror-defendants/370806141/.
2. Mitchell D. Silber and Arvin Bhatt. "Radicalization in the West: The Homegrown Threat," New York Police Department, 2007. Retrieved from http://sethgodin.typepad.com/seths_blog/files/NYPD_Report-Radicalization_in_the_West.pdf.
3. Brian Michael Jenkins. "Outside Experts View," preface to Daveed Gartenstein-Ross & Laura Grossman, *Homegrown Terrorists in the U.S. and U.K.: An Empirical Examination of the Radicalization Process*. Washington, DC: FDD's Center for Terrorism Research, 2009.
4. Peter Neumann. "Preventing Violent Radicalization in America," Bipartisan Policy Center, June 2011, p. 18. http://bipartisanpolicy.org/sites/default/files/NSPG.pdf.
5. Hanna Rosin. "How A Danish Town Helped Young Muslims Turn Away From ISIS," NPR, July 15, 2016. http://www.npr.org/sections/health-

shots/2016/07/15/485900076/how-a-danish-town-helped-young-muslims-turn-away-from-isis.

6. "Developing Counter-Radicalization Programs Against ISIS," The John Hay Initiative, January 14, 2016. http://www.choosingtolead.net/john-hay-blog/2016/1/14/developing-counter-radicalization-programs-against-isis-1.
7. Ibid.
8. Ibid.
9. Dina Temple-Raston. "Cyber Bombs Reshape U.S. Battle Against Terrorism," All Things Considered (radio), September 12, 2016. http://www.npr.org/2016/09/12/493654985/cyber-bombs-reshape-u-s-battle-against-terrorism
10. David E. Singer. "Obama Order Sped Up Wave of Cyberattacks Against Iran," *New York Times*, June 1, 2012, http://www.nytimes.com/2012/06/01/world/middleeast/obama-ordered-wave-of-cyberattacks-against-iran.html.
11. J. M. Berger and Jonathon Morgan. "The ISIS Twitter Census: Defining and Describing the Population of ISIS Supporters on Twitter," Center for Middle East Policy at Brookings. https://www.brookings.edu/wp-content/uploads/2016/06/isis_twitter_census_berger_morgan.pdf
12. Jim Acosta. "Government Enlists Tech Giants to Fight ISIS Messaging," CNN, February 25, 2016. http://www.cnn.com/2016/02/24/politics/justice-department-apple-fbi-isis-san-bernardino/.
13. Patrick Cockburn. "War with Isis: Islamic Militants Have Army of 200,000, Claims Senior Kurdish Leader," *Independent*, November 16, 2014. http://www.independent.co.uk/news/world/middle-east/war-with-isis-islamic-militants-have-army-of-200000-claims-kurdish-leader-9863418.html
14. Michael Lipka. "Muslims and Islam: Key Findings in the U.S. and Around the World," Pew Research Center, February 27, 2017. http://www.pewresearch.org/fact-tank/2017/02/27/muslims-and-islam-key-findings-in-the-u-s-and-around-the-world/
15. Laurie Goodstein. "Muslim Leaders Wage Theological Battle, Stoking ISIS' Anger," *New York Times*, May 8, 2016. https://www.nytimes.com/2016/05/09/us/isis-threatens-muslim-preachers-who-are-waging-theological-battle-online.html

GLOSSARY

Baghdadi, Abu Bakr al- The leader of ISIS, Baghdadi helped found al-Qaeda in Iraq, which would later become ISIS. Prior to his complete radicalization, Baghdadi was detained by US forces at Camp Bucca in Iraq, but was released in 2004. He has been serving as leader of the group now known as ISIS since 2010.

bay'ah A promise made by a citizen to the Islamic State and its leaders, promising that the person making the pledge will serve ISIS.

caliph A person who is considered to be a successor to the Muslim prophet Muhammad and the leader of the entire Muslim community.

caliphate A Muslim state that is governed by the laws of Islam and is run by a caliph. The caliphate run by ISIS is guided by Sharia law.

counterterrorism Tactics used to prevent the spread of terrorism. True counterterrorism efforts involve the military, government, intelligence agencies, and local communities working together to prevent terrorist attacks, as well as to keep citizens from joining terror groups.

Fatah ash-Sham A terrorist group linked to al-Qaeda and ISIS, but based in Syria. It is also called the al-Nusra Front.

Hadith In Islam, a Hadith is a report of the actions and sayings of the prophet Muhammad. Second only to the Quran, the Hadith are based on stories told about the prophet after his death.

hashtag On social media, hashtags are labels inserted after tweets or Instagram posts that allow users to view all posts on a specific topic. Hashtags are noted by the number sign (#) on social media.

homegrown terror Acts of terror that are carried out by a citizen of the country that is being attacked. Frequently, homegrown terrorists have never traveled abroad for terror training or activity and instead learn terror tactics online and then carry out their attacks on their neighbors.

Islam A religion that believes there is only one god, known as Allah, and that Muhammad is the final prophet. Islam is broken into a number of sects, much like Christianity is divided, and approximately 23 percent of the world follows this religion.

Islamic Front A Syrian terror group that seeks to overthrow the Syrian government and start its own Islamic state in Syria. Although they have similar goals, the Islamic Front has condemned ISIS for their attacks on innocents and other Muslims.

Islamic State Also called ISIS, ISIL, IS, or Da'esh, the Islamic State is a terror group that practices an extreme version of Islam and believes that Muslims should live in their own state, separate from the nonbelievers.

jihad In Arabic, "jihad" means "to strive" or "struggle," but in common usage it means "to fight a holy war for Islam."

Levant The Levant is a geographic region that covers parts of Europe, Asia, and Africa. Countries that make up the Levant are Cyprus, Israel, Iraq, Jordan, Lebanon, Palestine, Syria, and Turkey. ISIS, which does not believe in modern geographic borders, refers specifically to regions of Syria and Iraq as the Levant.

lone wolf Someone who acts on his or her own without being specifically ordered by a leader or group. In terms of terrorism, a lone wolf is an attacker who chooses and carries out his or her own attack in the name of ISIS, but who is not directed to do so by ISIS leaders and does not receive support from the greater ISIS organization.

Muhammad The prophet, or messenger from God, in the Islamic faith, as well as the de facto founder of Islam. Muhammad lived in the seventh century, and in 610 CE, he reported receiving a visit from the angel Gabriel, who delivered to him the word of God.

mujahideen People engaged in jihad. ISIS fighters can be referred to as mujahideen.

Muslims Followers of the Islamic faith.

niqab Worn by some Muslim women, and required of women in ISIS territory, a niqab is a veil that covers the wearer's entire face. The niqab is worn with a hijab, or headscarf, so that only the wearer's eyes can be seen.

Qaeda, al- A terrorist organization founded by Osama bin Laden and now run by Ayman al-Zawahiri, al-Qaeda is a militant Sunni group that was responsible for the September 11, 2001, attacks on the United States.

Quran The Islamic holy book. It is believed that the Quran is the word of God as told to Muhammad and written down by Muhammad's scribes.

radicalization The process by which someone adopts an extreme political, social, or religious ideology.

Radicalization requires outside influence, whether from a friend or family member, religious leader, or website.

Salafism An extremely conservative sect of Sunni Islam, Salafism began in the eighteenth century and requires the following of Sharia law.

Sharia law Islamic law derived from the writings in the Quran.

Sunna A collection of the teachings of Muhammad and one of the sources of Sharia, or Islamic law.

Taliban An extremist Muslim political group that forces followers to obey Sharia law.

Wahhabism An ultraconservative version of Islam, Wahhabism is named for its founder, Muhammad ibn Abd al-Wahhab. Wahhab believed that "religious innovation" was wrong and required followers to practice a puritanical version of Islam.

West The West is a catchall phrase used mostly to mean America, but that also includes Europe and Canada. The name is derived from "Western Hemisphere," where America and Europe are located. As it regards ISIS, the West is the enemy of the caliphate.

FURTHER READING

Books

Atwan, Abdel Bari. *Islamic State: The Digital Caliphate*. Oakland, CA: University of California Press, 2015.

Fishman, Brian H. *The Master Plan: ISIS, al-Qaeda, and the Jihadi Strategy for Final Victory*. New Haven, CT: Yale University Press, 2016.

January, Brendan. *ISIS: The Global Face of Terrorism*. Minneapolis, MN: Twenty-First Century Books, 2017.

Kennan, Caroline. *The Rise of ISIS: The Modern Age of Terrorism*. Farmington Hills, MI: Lucent Press, 2017.

Websites

Belfer Center
www.belfercenter.org
Run by Harvard's Kennedy School for Science and International Affairs, the Belfer Center offers detailed analysis on terrorism and war, not just in the United States, but around the globe.

New York Times
www.nytimes.com
This daily news website follows the news closely to allow you to keep up to date with what is happening in ISIS territory as well as with ISIS-inspired and ISIS-directed incidents around the world.

RAND
www.rand.org
A research organization, RAND studies terrorism and counterterrorism among other homeland security issues. Expert analysts offer commentary on not only the big picture of ISIS, but on recent incidents and attacks as well.

US Department of Homeland Security
www.dhs.gov
The US Department of Homeland Security offers up-to-the-minute news on security and terrorism issues facing the United States, as well as discussions about these topics from experts, politicians, and security officers.

INDEX

A

Aarhus method, 82
Adnani, Abu Muhammad al-, 15, 28
Amriki, Abu Issa al-, 59–60
Armageddon, 22, 41, 46
Ataturk, Mustafa Kemal, 14, 23

B

Baghdadi, Abu Bakr al-, 5, 6, 14–15, 20, 21, 22, 54, 60
bay'ah, 54
bin Laden, Osama, 35, 46, 47, 49
Boko Haram, 55, 83
boundaries, 26, 86

C

caliph, 14, 20, 22, 24, 54
caliphate, 7, 14–15, 17, 20, 22–23, 26–30, 33, 36, 48–49, 51, 55, 57, 59
Carter, Ashton, 79, 80
communications, 9, 30, 34, 66
community, 9, 14, 49, 58, 76–78, 82–83, 86
counterterrorism, 67, 82
cyber warfare, 79

D

Dabiq, 26, 30, 41

Davis, Michael, 73, 74
deradicalization, 73, 76, 82

F

Farook, Rizwan, 67
Fatah ash-Sham, 55
funding, 52–53

H

hacking groups, 42
Hadith, 11, 48–49
hashtag, 36–37, 41
Hayat Media Center, al-, 34–36
homegrown terror, 66

I

Islam, 7–8, 9, 11, 13–14, 16–17, 22–24, 26–27, 36, 41, 49, 54, 58, 67, 79, 86
Islamic Front, 55
Islamic State, 5, 7–8, 9–10, 13–19, 20, 22–23, 25–30, 31, 33–37, 40–42, 45, 48–49, 51–52, 54–55, 57–58, 59–60, 62–63, 66–67, 72, 73, 79, 83, 86–88

J

jihad, 5, 13, 16, 30, 48–49, 51, 57–58, 59, 73, 75, 82, 88

K

Kesinovic, Samra, 18–19
kidnapping, 52, 55

L

Levant, 5
lone wolf, 66–67

M

Malik, Tashfeen, 67
Management of Slavery, The, 40
martyr, 16, 49
Muhammad, 11, 14, 20, 22, 26, 28, 49, 54, 67
mujahideen, 46
muqadams, 62
Muslims, 5, 9, 11, 14–17, 20, 22–23, 25–26, 28, 31, 36, 40, 45–46, 48–49, 54, 63, 67, 72, 76, 78, 83, 86

N

Najd, 55
New York Police Department (NYPD), 76
niqab, 9, 19

O

Obama, Barack, 31, 32

P

propaganda, 34, 36–37, 41–42, 83

Q

Qaeda, al-, 7, 35, 40, 47–48, 54–55, 62–63, 86
Qaeda in Iraq, al- (AQI), 40, 47
Quilliam Foundation, 61
Quran, 11, 16, 24, 26, 33–34, 48–49
Qutb, Sayyid, 48

R

radicalization, 13, 17–18, 62, 66, 73–77
recruitment, 5, 9, 33, 35, 45, 72, 73, 86
refugees, 63, 70, 72
rehabilitation, 73, 75
revenue, 35, 51

S

Salafism, 24, 26
San'a, 55
Sharia law, 25, 28
Shia, 22, 28, 55, 63
Simpson, Elton, 67
smartphone apps, 5, 36, 42
social media, 5, 12, 19, 30, 36, 42, 83
Stuxnet, 87
Sunna, 11, 24
Sykes-Picot Agreement, 25

T

Taliban, 46–47
training, 30, 76

V

videos, 10, 25, 31, 33, 35, 41, 60

W

Wahhabism, 24, 26
West, 9, 13, 16–17, 26, 36, 40–41, 46, 49, 62, 72, 83
Wilayat Sinai, 55

Y

Yazdani, Mohammad Ibrahim, 59

Z

Zarqawi, Abu Musab al-, 7, 35, 40, 47